A Lazy Man's Guide to Success

Bill O'Hanlon

ISBN: 1468144510
ISBN-13: 978-1468144512

DEDICATION

To Helen and Rudy, who help me put the lazy back into the Lazy Man by giving me an incentive not to work so much.

CONTENTS

ACKNOWLEDGMENTS

Thanks to Werner Erhard, David Whyte and Milton Erickson for the inspiration. Thanks to my proofreaders/friendly critics: Bob Bertolino, Paul O'Hanlon, Deborah Altshuler, Shelly Jones, Rob and Cherry McNeilly, Marian Sandmaier, Lisa Munsat, Enid Jackowitz, Alan Hutner, Jonathan Udesky, Martha Geske, Jerry Jerome, Jerry Gammell (above and beyond the call of readership; glad I could help you find a productive use for your proofreading compulsion—I have one of those too, but it is hard to do it for my own work), Leslie Szent-Miklosy and Paul Lambakis (corrector extraordinaire). Couldn't have done it without ya. Don't know how those non-English sentences and all those typos got in there. Thanks for catching 'em. Thanks to Sandy Beadle for the digital makeover and easing this into its first print edition.

INTRODUCTION: A LITTLE BOOK ABOUT SUCCESS

"I couldn't wait for success . . . so I went ahead without it."
—Jonathon Winters

This is a little book about success. What I mean by success is accomplishing something you really want to accomplish in the world and getting others to support it and agree that it is of value. That, of course, is not the only definition of success, but it's my book and that's my definition. I wrote this book for people who are not yet clear about what it is they are supposed to do while they're on the planet and for those who do know, but haven't pursued their missions or dreams. This book will tell you everything you need to know to succeed. Not how to be happy. Not how to be a good person. Not how to be loved. Not even how to be wealthy. Those can be good things and they may be byproducts of success. But not necessarily. Sometimes success can even get in the way of being happy or a good person.

1

This book is about successfully realizing your passions, destiny or dreams if you know what they are. It's also about finding out what you are meant to do in this life if you don't know yet what that is.

Why did I call it *A Lazy Man's Guide to Success?* [Please note that it is not the sexist title that some of you thought at first glance—this is my story—I'm the lazy guy of the title.] Because I succeeded when I, and most folks around me, wouldn't have bet on me to succeed earlier in my life.

One day, my wife said to me in amazement, "You know, you are the laziest successful person I have ever known." I laughed and had to agree. I am the laziest successful person I know, too. I have written 35 books (Stop me before I write again!) that have been translated into fifteen other languages. I've been on Oprah (for some people, this is my main claim to fame). I teach workshops all over the world for thousands of dollars per day. I have created several methods and theories of psychotherapy that are practiced in various parts of the world. But you can't get me to do anything I am not interested in.

I'm terribly distractible. I rarely work except when I am required to in order to keep a commitment. I typically put off writing my books as long as I can. In college, I discovered I couldn't sign up for any classes that began before 11:30 a.m. because I would oversleep too often to pass the course. My office is a mess. Until recently, I always filed my taxes late, because I couldn't get it together to find all my receipts and take the time to fill out the forms—or even get them to an accountant. I prefer to sit around playing the guitar, reading, watching movies and hanging out at home.

A LAZY MAN'S GUIDE TO SUCCESS

I was certainly lazy and remain so. I didn't think I was strong enough, ambitious enough, or organized enough to make it. But I succeeded—beyond my wildest expectations. [Another inspiration for the title was a book I read years ago called *A Lazy Man's Guide to Enlightenment*.]

A few years ago, I had a sort of reverse midlife crisis, wondering how I had been lucky enough to live my dreams. I kept asking myself: Why have I succeeded, while others who are more talented, smarter and more self-disciplined have not? When I asked my wife this same question, she amended her previous observation. "Well," she said, "you are lazy and you aren't. When you get engaged, you work faster, better and with more focus than anyone I've known." And that's what this book is in part about. How do you succeed when you are lazy and undisciplined—or otherwise gifted at sabotaging yourself?

Were you one of those kids whose parents were always hearing that you weren't "working up to your potential"? If so, this book is definitely for you. It will also work for you annoying people who are self-disciplined and not lazy by any stretch of the imagination, but who haven't reached your goals because you don't know where to apply your self-discipline. Or for those of you who are so perfectionistic, you tend to get in your own way. Or those of you who are totally clueless about what you are meant to do with your lives.

So, here it is, the most succinct version I can give you of what I have learned about how to succeed. It's as short as I can make it and still make what I have to say compelling and clear.

Okay. Let me give you an overview of where we're going. First, we'll explore the importance of having a compelling dream or vision or direction to move in.

Next I'll tell you why you need a soul to succeed and what a soul is for (and this will have nothing to do with religion, so relax if you're religion-phobic). Even if you already know you have a soul, this chapter is worth reading (relax again, it's only a few pages), 'cause if you miss this, you're screwed. The rest of the book won't work.

If by the end of the chapters on dreams and soul, you don't already have a dream that matters enough to get off the couch and go after, then I'll give you some ideas about how to get a dream like that.

Next I'll tell you how to get the world to be your guru and teach you how to make your dream come true.

Last (well almost), I'll tell you why I think it is important to have a dream that is not just for your own personal gratification (like getting rich or getting laid or getting famous). Nothing wrong with wanting those things or getting them, but if that is your main motivation for success, again, you may be screwed.

Then I'll give you a one-page summary of the whole book. Those of you who are really lazy can just flip back there and get the gist of things and maybe it will work, but I doubt it. You'll probably actually have to read the book to really get it. Sometimes the devil, as well as God, really is in the details.

Last (really last this time), I've thrown in a pet theory of mine about how to arrange your work and money life so you can be lazy the rest of your natural born days, because you can arrange things so you don't do work you don't want to do, and have money come to you without putting in ongoing time or effort.

Ready? Place your tray tables to the upright and locked position. Keep your hands and arms inside the car. Here we go!

CHAPTER 1. YOU GOTTA HAVE A DREAM

In the musical South Pacific, there is a line in one of the songs: *You gotta have a dream, Cause if you don't have a dream, how're you gonna have a dream come true?* So if you haven't got a sense of where it is you are supposed to go in your life or you haven't got a dream, go get one. If you haven't got one yet, make one up that seems to have heart and interest for you. Pick as good a dream as you can get; one that energizes you.

It is not even crucial that you fulfill this dream, but you have to get your car out of the garage somehow and moving on down the road. It doesn't really even have to be a specific dream or goal. Maybe it's just a direction. Once you get out there, you may spy some nicer scenery, or figure out where you're really supposed to go, or change direction entirely.

When I was young and in college, I became very depressed. I thought myself a poet and was so sensitive that I found it

1

painful to be around people. At the same time, I was very lonely, and wanted to be around people. But when I was around people, I was so shy I couldn't say the things I wanted to say. Or when I would talk, I was so nervous I wound up saying something I didn't mean to say.

I began to despair about my future. Someday college would be over and I'd have to get a job. My poetry wouldn't support me, especially since I was too frightened of rejection to show it to anyone (not exactly an effective strategy for getting published). And I couldn't see myself behind a desk or a counter, or balancing on the rung of some corporate ladder.

After months of being depressed, I finally came to an important decision: I would kill myself. I had three close friends and they were generally as miserable and strange as I was, so I decided the only polite thing to do was to apprise them of my plans and say goodbye. The first two friends I told were sympathetic and told me they felt the same way but didn't have the guts to take their own lives. They admired my courage, though. My third friend became very upset when I told her of my suicidal plans (she was a bit more normal). When I explained my reasons, she made this offer. As the favorite niece of unmarried aunts in the Midwest, she stood to inherit some farms they owned. If I promised not to kill myself, my dear friend said, she would let me live in one of these houses, rent-free, for the rest of my life. I could write poetry, stay away from the world and people, and even grow my own food if I wanted (which, in my delusional state at the time I actually thought I could do).

The important thing is that it seemed like a possibility to me. I was instantly relieved of my suicidal feelings. I had a future with possibilities. I had a dream, a goal, a mission, a direction. Singer/songwriter Bruce Cockburn has a line in one of his songs: *In the absence of vision, there are nightmares.* I was living a nightmare because I had no vision of a better future, only one that was the same as or worse than, the present. My friend's kind offer had opened up a new future for me.

Of course, the next challenge was how to live until one of the aunts departed (they were in their sixties and, at 19, I was certain one of them was going to leave the planet within a few years—turns out they lived for many years after that). I was no longer going to kill myself, but I was still miserable. So, now I had a new mission—I became obsessed with discovering how people lived successfully, that is, how they weren't miserable all the time as I was, how they got along with other people, how they handled money.

CHAPTER 2. LET YOUR SOUL BE YOUR PILOT

In order to succeed, you are going to need your soul. That may sound a bit stupid, because you may be certain you already have a soul. And perhaps you do. But I will tell you what I mean by soul. I will tell you what a soul is good for and suggest ways to reclaim the bits of it that may be missing. I think people who have trouble succeeding have misplaced at least part of their souls.

What a Soul is Good for, Part I: Energy, Aliveness and Passion
Your soul is the place in your body, your self, or your life where your energy and vitality lives and grows. Generally, children seem to have their souls intact. They are vibrant and alive. They have boundless energy. Contrast that with most of us in our work. We're often exhausted before we even get there. The poet David Whyte jokes that when the alarm rings for us to get up and go to work, some part of us objects to going, so we leave about 50 percent of ourselves in bed. Off

we trudge to work, dragging ourselves out the door. But when we get to the parking lot, another 30 percent of us just refuses to go into that place. So we leave that bit of ourselves in the car, cracking a window so it won't suffocate while we are at work. Is it any wonder, he asks, you feel exhausted after a day at work?

Think of yourself as a circle. We start life as complete 360-degree selves, then we begin to cut away slices. As we make compromises, or try to fit in, or look for love or security, we wind up shaving off, smoothing out, cutting off, hiding or suppressing more and more of who we are. We end up with a 227-degree self or a 164-degree self.

So we kind of fit in, but each of those slices we left behind contained some of our basic life force or energy. YOU'RE GONNA NEED THAT ENERGY IF YOU WANT TO SUCCEED.

My wife has this thing she does with her hands when she is energized. She shakes them in a peculiar way, as if she is filled with energy and it is spilling out of her. I can always tell when she is excited or happy about something; the hands start to go. I sometimes howl or thrust my fist into the air and let out a whoop when I feel similarly energized. You probably have your equivalent, unless you're half dead at this point in your life.

What brings your soul alive and makes your heart sing? What excites you? What makes energy just run through your body? It's like that children's game in which some object is hidden, but the other participants are not allowed to tell you where it is. All they can do is tell you whether you are hot or cold as you wander around looking for it. If you are getting close, they say, "Warm." If you then move in the wrong direction, they say, "Colder, colder," but if you turn and begin to move in the right direction, they say, "Warmer, warmer, warmer, hot, hotter," as you approach the hidden object. Your soul plays the same game with you, letting you know by your energy level whether you are close or farther away from what brings you alive.

What a Soul is Good for, Part II: Integrity and Uniqueness

Let me clue you in, my dear reader—you are a deviant. And I mean that in a good way. I know you try to hide it, but it's true. If anyone really knew the weird thoughts, impulses and fantasies you have on a regular basis, they would lock you up, wouldn't they? Nobody else quite thinks and feels like you do. You are unique.

Being a psychotherapist (emphasis on psycho) for over a quarter century, I have been to that weird place with many people over the years. We're all freaks, and what's freaky about us is often what's best about us.

So the other function of the soul is to bring together all the diverse elements within you that make you unique, like your DNA does with your body. All of the abilities, skills and distinctive qualities that make your sensibilities and expressions like no one else's in the world are available through the integrity your soul brings to your life. Martha Graham, the legendary dancer/choreographer, said it well: "There is a vitality, a life force, an energy, a quickening that is translated through you into action—and because there is only one of you in all of time, this expression is unique. And if you block it, it will never exist through any other medium and be lost. The world will not have it. It is not your business to determine how good it is nor how it compares with other expressions. It is your business to keep it yours, clearly and directly."

What is it that only you can do in the way you can do it? What do you constantly try to smooth over about yourself or

6

dismiss as too bizarre or embarrassing? That's probably what you have to offer the world. Do you know Bobby McFerrin, the singer and now orchestra conductor? His big hit was "Don't Worry, Be Happy". He performed dressed only in jeans, bare feet and bare-chested, making odd noises issue from his body, by singing, humming, slapping his chest. His music was like no one else's. I'm sure when he first began singing that way, his friends and family chastised him: *Bobby, you are weird. Stop that or you'll never make it in music.* He seems to have done okay for himself.

I once heard a story about Leo Szilard, the physicist. One day he told a friend he had started keeping a diary. He wanted, he said, to record the facts for God. His friend chided him. "Leo, don't you think God already knows the facts?" "Yes," replied Szilard, "but not this version!"

Nobody has the same version, perception or expression of life you do. No one has the same store of experience or exact values and concerns you do. That is your gift, really all that you are—you are as unique as your fingerprints. As the poet e. e. cummings wrote: *To be nobody - But - Yourself - In a world which is doing its best night and day to make you everybody else - means to fight the hardest battle any human being can fight and never stop fighting.*

Part of your integrity is embracing the contradictions within yourself. When I was growing up, I was painfully shy. In my late twenties, because I was passionate about sharing some ideas and methods of therapy that excited me, I realized I would have to start teaching workshops and seminars. The problem was that I was shy. When I thought about it, I discovered that I had really bought into a myth about myself. I was shy most of the time, but on some occasions, I was not shy (with my close family members or friends, for example). So, the truth was I was shy and not shy (I have since discovered my inner ham, which loves to talk in front of people).

I am lazy and not lazy. I am a nice guy and a son of a . . . well, you get the point. As Walt Whitman wrote: *Do I contradict myself? Very well, then. I am large. I contain multitudes.* Can you contain the multitudes within you? Most people are not just one way. They contain contradictions. Again, if you try to smooth over or hide the contradictions, you make yourself smaller. Too small, perhaps, for what you will have to do to succeed.

As Marianne Williamson has written: "Your 'playing small' does not serve the world. There is nothing enlightened about shrinking so that other people don't feel insecure around you. We were born to make manifest the glory of God that is within us. It is not just in some of us. It is in everyone."

Susana Herrera, in her book, *Mango Elephants in the Sun*, recounts that in the rural Cameroonian village where she spent a two-year Peace Corps stint, they had a traditional greeting which went, *Jam bah doo nah?* (Are you in your skin?), which had the expected answer of *Jam core doo nay!* (I am in my skin!). That's really the question I have for you here: Are you in your skin?

A few years ago, I was giving a talk at a conference on treating people who had been sexually abused. During my presentation, I spoke about having been sexually molested by my grandfather. I used a lot of irreverent humor while relating this rather terrible and sad thing that happened to me when I was young. One of my friends and colleagues, Steve Gilligan, was in the audience of a few hundred people. During the question and answer period following my talk, Steve stood up, looked out over the audience and said simply, "Bill O'Hanlon is a deviant." There were a few nervous titters. "No, really," he went on. "No one else would have told that incident just the way Bill did. He is really unique. He's a deviant. But he seems so comfortable in his deviance, doesn't he? He is a good role model for being deviant and unashamed." I was very pleased with what Steve had said and for a while, considered getting myself a tee-shirt made that said DEVIANT AND PROUD.

A few months later, I was giving another talk and told that story. After the talk, a woman approached me with her own story. She had attended a class with a spiritual teacher who was visiting from India. She had been studying spirituality for many years and had meditated regularly. While she really enjoyed the class, the teacher used a phrase every week that had perplexed and troubled her. He kept repeating and emphasizing, "You must double your weirdness!" Whenever he used the phrase, it startled her. However, when she looked around the room at the other students, she saw them nodding their heads with enthusiasm and diligently taking notes. She spent the time between classes trying to understand this cryptic phrase, which seemed to have nothing to do with the rest of his teachings. She felt stupid, since everyone else seemed to be getting it rather easily. After about six weeks of classes, she had grown used to his thick Indian accent. One night she realized in a flash what he had been saying that whole time was really, "You must develop your awareness!"

She felt relieved and slightly silly for having struggled so with such a simple misunderstanding. But as she heard my story, she realized she had actually been hearing the message she most needed to hear for her spiritual growth. She was always concerned about fitting in and looking good and being "normal." She vowed that from that night on, she would work on "doubling her weirdness." So, that is your assignment, if you are willing to accept it. Embrace your deviance; double your weirdness.

The very things we try to smooth over or hide can be the things that propel us to success, because their energy and aliveness are available. Now when I use the words "weird" or "deviant," I hope you realize I am being dramatic to make a point.

Three Ways to Find or Reclaim your Soul

These integrative and energizing functions of the soul can provide the fuel for both finding your dreams and realizing them, because they help you discover and claim more of your aliveness and uniqueness. If you don't have full access to your soul, you will find it much harder (perhaps impossible) to discover what it is you want to do. Even if you do discover it, if you don't reclaim your soul, you won't have the energy to accomplish the things you need to accomplish to succeed. And if you hide your deviance and uniqueness, what you end up doing may not succeed because it will look like what anyone could have done. There are several ways to reclaim your energy, integrity and soul.

Here are three:
1. Pursue and follow what energizes you and brings you alive.
2. Embrace your deviance, your uniqueness, your voice.
3. Embrace and allow your seeming contradictions.

These then, are the two functions of your soul.
1. Energy, Aliveness, Passion - Soul gives energy and alerts us to when we're in the presence of energy-givers or energy-drainers as we move through life.
2. Integrity or Integration - Soul contains the contradictory and conflicting aspects of ourselves. Soul lets us know when we have integrity and when we are off the path of integrity.

CHAPTER 3. HOW TO GET A DREAM
WORTH PURSUING: BLISSED OR PISSED

When I teach seminars on this topic, participants often ask me how they can discover what their missions, destinies and dreams really are. At first, this stumped me a bit, because I'm one of those obnoxious people who already knows what he is supposed to be doing. I usually have too many dreams and have to settle on one or two at a time. I usually stumble or grope my way blindly into my future. I generally know when I'm on the right road and when I've gone astray—such as when I'm doing something just for fame or fortune. (Nothing wrong with fame and fortune, but things lose their meaning and aliveness for me when I do them only for personal gain. Maybe it will be different for you. But I doubt it.)

After observing and thinking about this for a while, I figured out something to say that might help people who don't find it so easy or automatic to find their dreams. So, here it comes.

Two ways to find a dream worth pursuing:

1. Follow your bliss, as mythologist Joseph Campbell once said. That is, attend to the stuff that excites you and brings you alive. Follow that. Keep doing it until something shows up that gives you the form that the world will appreciate and support (and ideally will pay you for as well, so you can pay the bills while pursuing your mission).

But this approach may not work for everyone. Some people come at the thing by a whole different route. For them, there is:

2. Follow what pisses you off or upsets you. What happens in the world that really bothers you? What evil do you want to correct? What is done in the wrong way that you think you might be able to change, given your abilities, your passion about the issue and what you have learned from your life experiences?

Some people seem to know instantly what blisses them out or pisses them off. Quincy Jones, the musician and record producer, tells in his autobiography, Q, about his transformation from delinquent to successful musician. He and some friends broke into a building intending to do some mischief and steal things. He came upon a room that was empty except for a piano. He was about to close the door to that room when something inside stopped him and told him to go in. He sat at the piano and began to play. From that moment on, he knew his life was going to involve playing music. Within a relatively few years, he was playing with some of the jazz greats of his time, Lionel Hampton and Frank Sinatra.

Business guru Tom Peters also knew. He co-wrote In Search of Excellence, which became an unexpected best-seller and revolutionized business practices around the world. Here's what he writes about it: "When I wrote [In Search of Excellence] . . . , I wasn't trying to fire a shot to signal a revolution. But I did have an agenda. My agenda was this: I was genuinely, deeply, sincerely, and passionately pissed off! So what's the point? Just this: Nearly 100% of innovation—from business to politics—is inspired not by 'market analysis' but by people who are supremely pissed off by the way things are."

Others seem to stumble their way along, living lives that are somehow wrong until they finally get it right. Dominick Dunne, the writer, was a Hollywood producer, doing relatively all right. But after some years at it, he realized even though he had fame and success, he didn't really like this life he thought he would love. He began to drink and use drugs to excess and got fired. "Thank God I hit bottom," he said, "Hitting bottom is a wonderful thing . . . If you can get back up."

After he was fired, a scandal erupted in Hollywood. A producer, David Begelman, was found to have forged a $10,000 check in the name of actor Cliff Robertson. Dunne followed the story in the papers and, having time on his hands, became obsessed with it. But the local papers soon swept it under the rug. Hollywood closed ranks and protected one of its own. The Washington Post got wind of the cover-up and sent two investigative reporters to Hollywood. But they couldn't get the close-knit Hollywood community to open up about the story. When one of them spotted Dunne in a restaurant (the reporter had gone to school with Dunne's brother), Dunne, being unemployed, having time on his hands, being interested in the story and knowing all the players in Hollywood, agreed to get the reporters entree into the Hollywood community. For two weeks, he accompanied them on their investigation. As he saw what investigative reporters did, he thought to himself,

"I can do this." He had always had it in the back of his mind that he would like to write and here was a direction.

Two other things made the direction much more clear. One was that Begelman essentially got away with few consequences from his misdeed (he was fired. as head of one big studio, but immediately hired as head of another), but Robertson, the victim, never had a major role in Hollywood after that. This mystified and upset Dunne.

Dunne's daughter was brutally murdered and something similar occurred. Dunne attended the trial and was appalled that the murderer seemed to have been coached on what to wear and how to act (he carried a Bible and read it constantly during the trial). Dunne knew enough from his time in the movies to recognize acting and props when he saw them. He became outraged as the trial proceeded when he saw that people with money and fame do not get the same legal consequences for bad deeds as do the rest of us.

He realized he could spend the rest of his life angry and embittered, but then a light came on. He could become an investigative reporter, specializing in writing about the rich and powerful in legal settings. "I had never had an interest in justice," he decried, "I was the guy who would rather be at the party." But now he was obsessed with justice. He left Hollywood and moved to a one-room shack in Oregon to write. He has made a good living at it ever since and has illuminated the injustice that often occurs when the rich and powerful are often able to get away with murder because of their fame, wealth and connections.

Follow Your Bliss
Okay, first the bliss. Here's poet Pablo Neruda, writing about the moment when he discovered poetry as his life's work: *something ignited in my soul, fever or forgotten wings.* What ignites your soul? What excites you when you anticipate doing or

14

pursuing it? Doesn't matter what it is. It could be doing crossword puzzles. It could be reading pornography. It could be contra-dancing. It could be movies. It could be knowing who played bass or drums on old rock songs. I have a friend who loves to figure out how to do several tasks as efficiently as possible in terms of time and motion. He takes great delight in plotting the most efficient route for the several errands he has to do. When he comes to visit me, he creates templates on my computer that simplify and automate the tasks I routinely do. This makes him happy (and me too).

Whatever that thing is, keep following it. Do not worry about figuring out how to make money or a career from it. We'll deal with that later. Just follow it. As much as you desire. I call these kinds of passions *soulful* obsessions, to distinguish them from those other kind of addictions and obsessions that destroy or diminish our souls and lives. Soulful obsessions sometimes involve huge amounts of work, but they seem effortless because we come alive and lose time when we engage in them.

When I was writing this book, I came across an interview in Rolling Stone magazine with musician Mark Knopfler, who had achieved fame and success with his group Dire Straits and as a solo artist. He was asked if he was obsessive about music. He responded, "You've got to be slightly obsessive about a job to be good at it. I used to smell Fender catalogs. (For non-music freaks, Fender is a brand of guitars.)" I thought that was great. I felt the same kind of obsessiveness in my pursuit of psychotherapy at first If you are as lazy as I am, this is a key point. I "work," I guess, but because I am so turned on by the things I do, I don't have to force or discipline myself to work. I can't wait to do the things I do. I become slightly obsessed with them.

I met a 7-year-old girl recently (while I was waiting for a medical appointment) who was constantly singing. I was charmed by the singing. When I remarked on this to her mother, I learned that this little girl knew the lyrics to hundreds of songs by heart. Her mother told me that sometimes she has to sing her requests and instructions to the girl to get her to do things. "Please pick up your toys," her mother croons. "Tiiiime for dinner," mother sings. Maybe that little girl will grow up following her passion for music or maybe others will stifle this quirky habit by telling her to be quiet and grow up.

That kid who drops out of Harvard to write software may turn out to be Bill Gates. That boy who secretly draws cartoons in class every chance he gets may turn out to be Walt Disney. That girl who can imitate anyone she meets may grow up to be Whoopi Goldberg. No guarantee, of course. But it's guaranteed if they don't pursue it, they won't get where those people got. The same goes for you.

Many people don't follow their passions because they can't imagine how they will make a living at them or because other people convince them there is no future or practical value in them. Most people would say that dropping out of Harvard is not practical.

You might be ashamed of what you enjoy, imagining that it is weird or trivial or stupid (or having been told that it is one of those things). Ray Bradbury writes of having torn up his prized collection of comic strips when he was a young boy because his friends mocked him and told him they were for babies. He immediately regretted his actions and vowed he would never let people shame him into betraying his interests again. Pursuing these comics and other weird passions (for example, he was obsessed with circuses and science fiction), he became a prolific writer. He maintains that following these strange interests without shame was the mother-lode of passion he tapped into that allowed him to be so productive and creative.

16

As Bradbury discovered, if you give this thing up or don't follow it, you may kill off that part of you. Then you would lose that bit of energy from your soul as well as precious time when you could be developing skills, knowledge, confidence or networks of relationships in that area. This is one of the tough parts about pursuing real success: other people will often disapprove of your actions and think your obsessions are silly and time-wasting. To keep their criticisms from stopping you in your tracks, you will probably have to develop a bit of rhino skin (or else pursue your passion in secret until it is strong enough to stand up to other people's naysaying). Remember this point: You need thick skin to follow your bliss.

If you truly follow your bliss, in time you will arrive some place that no one can reach. I once heard a story about Neil Young, the singer/songwriter. With many other Canadian singers, he was participating in a benefit recording, the Canadian version of "We Are the World," for hunger relief. Each artist had his or her own line to sing. During the playback, the producer stopped the tape after Neil Young's line and said rather sheepishly, "Neil, you were slightly off-pitch. Let's do it over." To which Young countered: "Hey, man, that's my style!" When I heard that story, I thought, *Now that's a man who has found his voice.* If you follow your bliss, you will find your own unique version of the thing you do and find your singular voice. No one will be able to steal what you have or do, because it is too much you. No one can do exactly what Bob Dylan, Lilly Tomlin, Neil Young, Bobby McFerrin, Laurie Anderson, James Joyce, Miles Davis or other deviants do best.

Blessed

Another aspect of being blissed is to identify by whom and about what you were blessed. Who has blessed us about something; someone who told you that you were good at something, believed in you, supported you at crucial and difficult moments, or mentored you? For example, was there a teacher who praised your writing; an uncle who thought you could sing amazingly; a friend who told you you were a great listener and should be a therapist; a parent who believed in you and told you you could do anything you set your mind to?

A professional colleague of mine, Patrick Carnes, told a story about growing up in an abusive dysfunctional family and church. He escaped into reading. The librarian at school noticed his interest and encouraged it. She saved books especially for him. She was his librarian and supporter through much of grade school and all through high school, where she transferred to a new job the year he began his high school years. Because of her blessing him, giving him the sense he was smart and good, he went on in his education, ultimately obtaining his Ph.D. and writing many books.

Pissed Off

Now for the pissed.

When I became a therapist, I was excited about finding ways to help people move from painful lives that didn't work to happier, more workable lives. To that end, I read voraciously, attended lots of workshops and got advanced training in methods and theories that I thought were especially effective. But I began to notice that my colleagues didn't pursue results as relentlessly as I did and often blamed their clients when they didn't get results. This upset me so much that sometimes, shy as I was, I suggested that perhaps the lack of results derived from the fact that they weren't using the latest and most effective techniques and ideas. My colleagues didn't appreciate my critiques and weren't moved to learn the new ideas and methods I was excited about. Soon I gave up saying anything. I realized that the way to move people was to become well known by teaching workshops and writing books about my ideas. After all, the people that had influenced me were people who taught and wrote and were well known in the field. So I set out to do that. Believe me, it was a challenge for me, a shy person and a novice writer who was usually too antsy to sit down and write, to commit to becoming a public speaker and a published author. But I was so pissed off about the disrespectful and ineffective approaches of my colleagues, and so moved by my clients' pain, that I was compelled to do it.

Candy Lightener, the founder of Mothers Against Drunk Driving (MADD), had a daughter who was killed by a drunk driver with multiple drunk driving arrests and convictions. She became so angry that she created a national movement that has changed drunk driving laws in the United States, prodded police and courts to better enforce existing laws, and saved thousands of lives. She couldn't bring her daughter back, but she could find some sense of meaning and purpose and save many other parents from going through what she had to go through.

Now when I say pissed, I mean something more than angry as well. It might be something that has hurt or wounded you that drives your passion and destiny. We all know the archetypal business tycoon who grew up dirt poor and hungry. One of my mentors, the psychiatrist Milton Erickson, grew up on a farm and always thought he would become a farmer himself until he was stricken with polio in his teens. When he found he no longer had the physical ability to farm, he knew exactly what he wanted to do: be a doctor. When he was a youngster, he developed an abscessed tooth. The infection became worse and worse, until one day it became unbearable. Erickson walked five miles to the doctor's office. The moment the doctor lanced the abscess, Erickson felt instant relief from that terrible pain. Then the doctor found out that the young boy had walked miles alone in pain and gave him a nickel. To a boy in the early 1900s, that seemed like a fortune. Not only was his pain gone, he had a nickel and felt happy. Somewhere in the back of his mind, Erickson decided that if one wasn't a farmer, then being a doctor was a great thing to do: to relieve pain and help people feel good was a noble calling.

It might be the opposite of being blessed. Who cursed you? Who told you you were not capable, good, or worthy? This gives us energy to prove them wrong or overcome our own secret fear that they were right in their pronouncements.

"You'll never make anything of yourself," says your stepdad, and years later, you drive up in your new Mercedes to show him he was wrong. Or you win the Pulitzer Prize and send a copy back to that editor who told you you couldn't write your way out of a paper bag.

I was reading an interview recently with the author of the children's book series, Captain Underwear. He was a poor student with some learning disabilities and many of his teachers and principals were harsh with him and made dire pronouncement regarding his future chances in this world. He is getting his revenge now by making "screw-up" students the heroes of his books (which have sold in the millions) and a principal the dupe for these students.

Pissed and Blissed
Sometimes a dream emerges from a mix of pain and passion. A colleague of mine, Ernest Rossi, had a learning disability that made it difficult for him to learn to read. Because learning disabilities were unheard of during his boyhood, when he fell seriously behind the other children, he was taken out of his classes and put with the kids who were called "retarded." On the playground, his former classmates teased him mercilessly, chanting "Ernie's a retard, Ernie's a retard." He was terribly ashamed.

A LAZY MAN'S GUIDE TO SUCCESS

When Ernie entered high school, his family had moved, and he had a chance to escape his old shame. Though he could now read, on that first day of high school, he began to doubt himself. *Maybe I'm not smart enough to hack it in high school,* he thought. After classes were over, he wandered around the big school library, feeling overwhelmed by all the knowledge contained in those books. His attention was caught by one particular thick tome. *If I could ever read a book like that and understand it,* he told himself, *it would prove I wasn't stupid.* He plucked it out of the stacks and read the title: *A Critique of Pure Reason,* by Immanuel Kant. He sat down to read it. He stared at the first paragraph and could not make heads nor tails of it. He read it again. And again. And again, until he finally understood what the author was saying. He did the same with the rest of the first page and finally, after understanding it, walked home with a deep feeling of satisfaction. Ernie visited the library every day after school and read that book until he had understood the whole thing. By the time he had graduated from high school, he had read the book three times.

Ernie went on to college and graduate school. While pursuing his Ph.D. in pharmacognosy (don't ask, it has to do with plants and medicines), a fellow Ph.D. student came to him one day and thrust a book in his hand and said, in effect: *Ernie, you are really messed up and need to read this book. It will help you.* Ernie looked up from his microscope, puzzled, and examined the thick book: *Interpretation of Dreams,* by Sigmund Freud. He took the book home, opened it, and immediately fell under its spell. You should know that Ernie is a very introverted guy and has a rich inner life. Here was a map of that inner life. The book completely captured him, so much so that he read it again and again (sound familiar?) Ultimately, he decided to drop out of his pharmacognosy program and to get a Ph.D. in psychology. He went on to become a Jungian analyst. Fascinated with dreams, Ernie created a new method of working with them, wrote a book about it, and developed a successful practice in southern California.

Things went along fine until some of his patients told Ernie that when they worked with him on their dreams, they felt that they had gone into trances. Ernie was upset by this. He was doing Jungian work and considered hypnosis a cheap parlor trick. But, as time went on, more and more patients mentioned this to him. One day, one of Ernie's most respected patients, a wise older man who knew a lot about Jungian work, also mentioned that Ernie's dreamwork was very hypnotic. After they discussed it, the man gave Ernie a book to read: *Advanced Techniques of Hypnosis and Therapy: Selected Papers of Milton H. Erickson, M.D.* Ernie took the book home at the end of the day, which happened to be a Friday. As before, he opened the book curiously and once again found himself captured. This fellow Erickson had an amazing way of working that was entirely different from the way Ernie had been taught. He spent all weekend reading the book. He was so excited about what he was reading, he barely slept until Sunday night.

Early on Monday morning, Ernie awoke with a severe stomachache. It was so painful that it drove him to go to the emergency room, where he was put through many tests. The tests found no physical cause for the pain and Ernie and the doctors finally concluded that it must be psychosomatic (perhaps he was unable to digest the fact that this book was going to challenge his old way of working and require him to learn a whole new approach). With the help of some medication, Ernie was able to return to his practice, though he was still in some pain. Meanwhile, he remained so impressed by Erickson's work that he made an appointment to see him, hoping that this eminent healer might help him resolve his now chronic stomach pain.

As he was driving from California to Phoenix, Arizona, where Erickson practiced, his stomach pain mysteriously disappeared. He arrived and told Erickson his story and they decided that Ernie would study with Erickson. They ultimately worked together on three books in which Ernie explained how Erickson did what he did, analyzing Erickson's work in detail like he did Kant's book and then dreams. Ernie has gone on to write many books about mind-body healing and related topics.

My point is that, in some ways, Ernie's life work derived mainly from a mix of his pain and self-doubt and his bliss. He seems to have proved by now (in his 60s) that he is not stupid (he assured me recently that he has now settled the issue within himself), but he followed both what upset him (proving he wasn't stupid by persisting with difficult material; following his stomachache to Erickson; mind-body healing) and his bliss (dreams and Erickson's work)

So, if you haven't got a dream that compels you yet, search in one or both of these directions:
What turns you on, blisses you out, excites you, compels you?

What do you seek out without any prodding from guilt or duty?

OR

What pisses you off? What has hurt you so much that you want to prevent it from happening to others?

Here are some questions that might help you find your destiny or dream.

HOW TO FIND OR RECOGNIZE
LIFE MISSIONS AND DESTINY

Increased energy
What gives you a sense of aliveness, energy and possibility?
What activities energize you, even though you have exerted yourself or worked at them?

Attentional fascination
What captures your attention or holds you spellbound?
What do you continue to return to when you have some time?
What do you make time to do or seek out even when you are busy?
What do you daydream about?

Righteous indignation
What would you talk about if given an hour of prime time television to influence the nation or the world?
What pisses you off that you would like to correct in the world or other people?

Soulful (not petty) envy/jealousy
What are others doing that you think you could make a better or more profound contribution doing a similar thing?

Recognizing this as your place or work
Where or what have you done that feels "just right"?
What feels like you were born to do it or where you were born to be?

Role models
Whose work or life do you admire?
Who inspires or moves you?

A LAZY MAN'S GUIDE TO SUCCESS

Blessings
Where were you blessed and about what?
Who blessed you?
What do I do with this information?

Right now, you don't have to figure out what to do with these signals. We'll get to that later. Right now we are discussing identifying the energy that calls or speaks to you.

Fill in any or all of this that is relevant to you.

Answering some of these questions can help you become more clear about the energy or energies that are moving in your life right now and that can help you find your direction and perhaps your life work.

When I read books with exercises or questions, I never do them. So why have I put some questions and exercises in this book? First, because some people actually do them and like them. But even if you're in my camp, I suggest you take the time and effort to answer any of these questions that speak to you, because just reading them won't do it. You've got to find a way to engage with this stuff. So, put down the bong, turn off the TV, and actually think over your answers, maybe even write them down.

Questions for exploring Bliss
Here are some questions to answer that might ferret out your bliss:
What activities do you seek out regardless of money or time constraints?
What do you love doing?
What can't you stop reading about?
Talking about?
Researching?
What do you want to tell people about because you're so excited about it?

What are or have been your soulful obsessions?

By this I don't mean the people you have stalked or the addictive activities that you have engaged in compulsively, but something that seemed inexplicable and also very deep. During college, I was obsessed with finding all the different versions of old English folk songs and copying them into my notebooks. I couldn't really explain my interest and at times, I neglected my university studies to pursue this interest. Many years later, when I became a writer, I realized that my soul was preparing me to be a writer by appreciating words and the slight variations of wording that can make all the difference.

Later, I became obsessed with reading computer magazines. I'm not much of a tech guy and was initially baffled by this interest, but years later, when I began to use my computer for writing books, doing computer-based slide presentations for my workshops, and creating e-books and audio products, I was able to do this without being intimidated by the technology.

What soulful obsessions have grabbed you?
What kind of books do you read compulsively?
What kind of activities do you engage in compulsively that don't seem unhealthy?
What kind of information do you seek out obsessively?
Who are you fascinated with?
What kind of gossip grabs you?
What riveted reactions have you had when:
Watching television?
Listening to the radio?
Talking to friends?
Something happens at work?
What parts of these activities or what activities have you enjoyed in the areas of:
Hobbies (past or present)?

A LAZY MAN'S GUIDE TO SUCCESS

Family activities?
Spiritual or religious activities?
Volunteer activities?
Career activities?
Vacations and trips?
Questions for exploring Blessed
Who has believed in you and encouraged you?
Who has told you that you were capable of something?
Who has been your inspiration or role model that got you to consider doing something in life or as a career?
Who is always on your side or in your corner?
When were you in the right place at the right time?
What natural abilities have you been blessed with?
What comes easily and naturally for you in life?

Questions for exploring Pissed
What critical, upset or angry reactions have you had when:
Watching television?
Listening to the radio?
Talking to friends?
Something happens at work?
What do you want to tell people about because you're so pissed off or indignant about it?
Did any of these activities have annoyances to them that you might feel moved to correct or tell people about?
Hobbies (past or present)
Family activities?
Spiritual or religious activities?
Volunteer activities?
Career activities?
Vacations and trips?

Questions for exploring Dissed
Where have you been dissatisfied in your life?
When or where have you or someone you cared about been disrespected or treated badly?
When were you envious about:

Someone's job?
Someone's accomplishment?
Someone's recognition?

CHAPTER 4. HOW TO MAKE YOUR DREAM COME TRUE: LET THE WORLD TEACH YOU WHAT WORKS

"The road to success is marked with many tempting parking spaces."
—Executive Speechwriter Newsletter

Once you know what you need to do, it's time to take action. Not just a little action, but as motivational guru Tony Robbins puts it, massive action. When you begin to pursue your success, unless you are extremely lucky or some mutant prodigy, most of your actions won't yield the results you want. The world will roundly ignore you. Your best-laid plans will go awry. Your friends, co-workers and family may think you are wacko and irresponsible and try to stop you from pursuing your crazy, unrealistic dream. (Remember rhino skin?) You have little or no evidence that your dream will succeed and little or no credibility with others. But you must begin to take action. It's the only way the world can teach you what works and what doesn't as you tread your path to success. You will do things and the world will reflect back to you whether or not they led you in the desired direction. You will also acquire more skills and knowledge in the area in which you take action. The 19th century cultural critic John Ruskin said it well: "What we think, or what we know, or what we believe is, in the end, of little consequence. The only consequence is what we do." Socialist theorist Freidrich Engels said it in another way: "An ounce of action is worth a ton of theory." Or how about this wisdom found in a fortune cookie: "Man must sit in chair with mouth open for very long time before roast duck fly in."

How to Fail Forward into Success

The only way to accomplish your dream in the face of such odds and resistance is to be willing to fail a lot. Keep trying stuff, notice the results, and try that thing again or try something else. Sometimes it fails only because you haven't shown you can persist or that you really believe in it. Sometimes it fails because it's just not the pathway to success. As W. C. Fields was once reputed to have said, "If at first you don't succeed, try, try again. If you still don't succeed, give up. There's no point in making a damned fool of yourself!" I translate this to mean: if what you are doing doesn't work after many tries, try doing it in a different way or try something else. (I believe in this approach so much that I wrote a whole book about it called *Do One Thing Different.*)

Recently I read an article about a new Internet-based advertising agency that adopted this motto: Figure out what sucks, then don't do that! The only way to figure out what sucks is to keep trying things. Some of them will suck (that is, fail to move you in your desired direction) and some of them will not suck. The founder of IBM, Thomas J. Watson, Sr., had this to say: "The fastest way to succeed is to double your failure rate." Ralph Waldo Emerson wrote: "All life is an experiment. The more you experiments you make the better." Hockey star Wayne Gretzky: "You miss 100% of the shots you never take." Novelist Louis L'Amour: "You can't learn anything from experiences you're not having."

But it's not enough to merely act. You have to pay attention to what happens as a result of your actions and make adjustments for your next action or set of actions. If you don't, you may just be flailing about, not necessarily moving forward. My teacher Milton Erickson said, "If you fall on your face, at least you're heading in the right direction." Playwright Samuel Beckett captured the flavor of this when he wrote: "Ever tried? Ever failed? No matter. Try again. Fail again. Fail better." Or this from Oswald Avery: "Whenever you fall, pick something up."

While I was writing this book, I saw a documentary about Gordon Parks. Gordon Parks is an African-American photographer (and novelist, and composer, and filmmaker and . . . well, you get the picture, he's a renaissance man). He told the story of how he became a photographer. He was working as a porter on a train, traveling around America. On one of his stopovers, he went to a museum. He saw an exhibit of photographs. He had never realized that photos could be art and these captivated him. From the museum, he went to see a movie. A newsreel was shown before the movie. The newsreel concerned a ship that had been attacked (it was during World War II) and the photographer who had recorded the bombing happened to be in the movie theatre and stood up and gave a short talk. He got a round of applause and Gordon Parks was deeply impressed. *(Here's the first hint from his soul—he was fascinated by the photos in the museum and by the fact that an ordinary person took famous photos and got recognition and praise. Something in him responded to those things.)*

On his next stopover, he went to a pawnshop and bought a camera. *(Here's the next hint: he took action. Now, he didn't yet have a plan to make money or a career of it, but he followed his bliss.)* He began to take photographs and sent some to Eastman Kodak, the camera and filmmaking company. *(Another hint: He took more action and let the world know what he was up to so it could teach him something and vote yes or no.)* The folks at Eastman Kodak told him that they liked his photographs and that, if he made some more, they would put together an exhibit. He did and they did. *(He was gathering evidence from the world that he was good at what he did.)*

One day, he got the idea that he would like to shoot fashion. He walked into a high-priced clothing store in Minneapolis, where he lived. The white owner of the store came out and suspiciously asked him what he wanted. He explained that he wanted to take fashion photos. The man derisively told him that that kind of photography was done in New York and Paris, not locally, and to leave the store. *(He could have walked out of the store at that moment having learned something. That would have been another step on the path. All because he took action.)* Just then, the owner's wife emerged from the back of the store and asked her husband what Parks wanted. The husband explained, and because the woman was upset with her husband about some tiff they had had, she told Parks to return to the store that evening and she would have some models waiting for him to photograph.

Parks then called a friend who had a better camera and lighting than he did and asked to borrow the friend's equipment for the night. His friend was amazed that Parks had taken on the assignment never having used such a camera or done fashion shoots before, but he came through with the equipment. Parks took many photos, but when he went home and developed them, found that he had double exposed all of them—except one. He asked his friend to help him develop that one photo and blow it up.

A LAZY MAN'S GUIDE TO SUCCESS

The next morning, Parks was waiting in front of the shop when the owners arrived. He had set up the one photo on an easel in front of the store. It was beautiful and the woman told him so. When she asked about the other photos, Parks honestly admitted that he had messed them up. She said, "Come back tonight and you can take some more." *(Parks didn't wait until he knew everything or the conditions were perfect before he acted. He was willing to make mistakes and learn on the job.)*

Soon Parks' fashion photos became well known and he was working steadily for *Vogue* and other fashion magazines. He was making a living doing something he loved. Then he decided that he wanted to work for *Life* magazine, the most famous photo magazine in the world at that time. (Happily, they also paid well, since Parks had a wife and kids to support.) He knew he would never get an appointment, being a black man and not having much of a reputation as a documentary photographer. So he found out where the photo editor's office was and simply walked in one day. When the editor asked him if he had an appointment, he admitted that he didn't. "How did you get in here without one?" the man asked. "I just walked in," Parks replied. "Well, then, you can walk the hell out right now." Parks said, "Come on, since I am here, won't you at least take the time to look at one or two of my photos?" The man reluctantly agreed. He hastily grabbed the photos and began flipping through them, but quickly stopped and began to look at them more carefully. "These are pretty good," he told Parks. Parks soon had a job at Life, and within a year, he was assigned to the magazine's Paris bureau, a plum assignment that usually took years to get. *(Hint: He took action. He gathered evidence of his ability. He made another convert to his dream. He got more and more evidence that his dream was real.)*

Now Parks could have been thrown out of the fashion store. He could have been thrown out of the office at *Life*. But he wasn't. (He didn't tell the stories of his frustrating failures to get anyone to give him a chance, but I'm sure there were many.) He didn't have a grand plan in mind when he got that first camera. He just kept following what excited and grabbed him and putting it out into the world. He messed up on his first fashion shoot, but that didn't him from stop taking action. He was a black man in racist America. *That didn't stop him from taking action.* He didn't know what he was doing. *That didn't stop him from taking action.* He didn't know how to make money from this thing he loved. *He found out!*

The only way to fail permanently is to stop. Otherwise, the experiment continues and possibilities remain. If you are willing to persist, observe, be flexible and stay in action, you will almost certainly arrive eventually. Will Rogers joked: "Even if you're on the right track, you'll get run over if you just sit there."

In 1961, President John F. Kennedy made a bold declaration: "We (the USA) will put a man on the moon within ten years." Many people got excited about this mission and signed on to help make it come true. But there also were naysayers; people who thought this dream was impossible. The people who were into making it happen asked the naysayers: "Well, *what* makes it impossible?" The naysayers replied that there was no metal available to withstand the heat of re-entry into the atmosphere. So we could send a man to the moon but we couldn't bring him back alive. The yeasayers then got busy, gave out research and development grants, and in time, such a metal was developed. Then the naysayers said: "Okay, maybe you overcame that hurdle but we still don't have the computing capability to chart a course and then adjust it quickly enough. The results would be needed in hours or minutes." More grants, more developments. The silicon chip. Faster computers. Then the naysayers again: "Okay, but..."

A LAZY MAN'S GUIDE TO SUCCESS

When you are committed to a dream and willing to take action, every naysayers and failure can actually further your progress. Bring them on. They can teach you what you need to deal with and overcome next. You can learn what didn't work or what others do not understand yet. Barriers are only problems if they discourage you enough to stop taking action. Otherwise, as writer Paul Hawken quips, *Problems are opportunities in drag.*

Don't Go with your Feelings

An important point here is that once you begin to act on your vision/direction/goal/ mission, do not go with your feelings. As a therapist, I actually love to tell this secret to people. Do not get in touch with your feelings and do not go with them when you are going for success. Now that is a little overstated, but I want to make a dramatic point, so I am going to overstate. What I mean is that most people stop in their tracks because they listen to and obey their fearful, doubtful feelings. If a little voice tells you that you are a fraud or your fear threatens to stop you, just tell that voice or the fear, "Thanks for sharing," and carry on.

Ray Bradbury, the eminent and productive science fiction writer, was once giving a talk to college writing students when one of them asked: "Mr. Bradbury, I find that sometimes I just don't feel inspired to write. How can I get myself in the writing mood?" Bradbury looked down at the student from the podium and replied, "Sit down and write, son. It will take care of all those moods you are having." Another writer, Peter DeVries, quips: "I write when I'm inspired, and I see to it that I'm inspired at nine o'clock every morning."

Obviously, if your feelings or thoughts are helpful ones that put wind in your sails, then by all means get in touch with them and go with them. But if they tend to mire you in fear, doubt and procrastination, take brief note of them and move on.

The other thing about your feelings is that they will probably get hurt in the course of pursuing your dream. In 1982, I did a workshop in Syracuse, New York, for about 125 people. Before leaving, the organizers asked if I wanted to read the feedback forms, so they wouldn't have to send them on to me. Most of them were complimentary, but three or four were pretty critical. One said, "Bill O'Hanlon is glib and articulate, but shallow. I thought this workshop sucked." Ouch! All the way home on the plane, I was upset. *I'm not going to do workshops any more. People are too mean. All I am trying to do is help people. I don't need this.* Luckily, I had a two-hour flight, an hour layover, and another two-hour flight to get home. By the time I was on my second flight, I had gotten some perspective. *Wait a minute, Bill, 120 of those people liked the workshop and got value out of it. A few people didn't. So what? Get a grip!*

People have attacked me in public and in print.

When I wrote in a book chapter that I was out to change the way psychotherapy was practiced in the world, a reviewer suggested that I was grandiose.

I once had a psychiatrist write to several publishers and urge them never to publish any of my future books because he claimed that I was anti-Semitic. He had misread a section in one of my books (and unbeknownst to this critic, my co-author for that book was Jewish, so I am sure he would have caught any anti-Semitism). I was upset at this mischaracterization and worried that someone might actually take it seriously as he flung his accusation far and wide.

Another time an influential therapist became upset with me and wrote to sponsors he knew and suggested they stop sponsoring me (which most did).

I worried initially that those attacks would hurt or destroy my career. They didn't. But they certainly were upsetting and anxiety-producing when they first happened.

If you have a dream and are going to put it out into the world, people will criticize you, misunderstand you and occasionally try to thwart or destroy you. So you had better develop some rhino skin (or stay sensitive and don't let your hurt feelings stop you). The formidable artist Georgia O'Keeffe said: "I've been absolutely terrified every moment of my life and I've never let it keep me from doing a single thing I wanted to do."

Faith, Agreement and Evidence: Kierkegaard, Indiana Jones and Picasso

There is a moment in *Indiana Jones and the Last Crusade* in which Indy is confronted with an impossible situation. He and his father (played by Sean Connery) have been searching for the Holy Grail so they can find it before the evil archeologist finds it and uses it to help the Nazis win the war. The Grail has the power to heal so if the Nazis get it, they could use it to cure their wounded.

Indy, his father and their friend are captured by the bad guys at the entrance to the passageway that leads to the Grail. The bad guys send some soldiers down the passageway to get the Grail but they are quickly killed as they fall prey to the traps designed to keep the Grail safe. The head bad guy realizes that only Indy is clever enough to get through the traps and orders him at gunpoint to retrieve the Grail. Indy refuses, declaring that the man will have to kill him. But the bad guy is smarter than that. He turns and shoots Indy's father, mortally wounding him so that he will die in short time if

Indy does not get the Grail. Indy, of course, cannot let his father die. (He's also got a bit of unfinished business with Dad—don't we all?)

Indy uses his guidebook, which has cryptic clues in Latin, to avoid most of the traps, but he finally comes to the edge of a deep chasm too wide to leap across. The guidebook shows a man stepping out into thin air, suggesting that one should have faith and step out. Now Indy is brave but he's not stupid. He tosses a pebble into the chasm and cannot even hear it hit the bottom. Just as he decides to turn back, his father's friend yells, "Indy, come quickly. Your father is dying. He won't last much longer. You must bring the Grail." So, closing his eyes, Indy steps out. He falls . . . just a few feet. The camera angle changes and we can see a walkway that has been so cleverly designed that it appears invisible, blending perfectly into the far wall of the canyon. Indy walks across, and, after a few more adventures and crises, saves the day.

Kierkegaard said much the same thing as Indy learned. You must take a leap of faith. (First time you've read a book that cites both Kierkegaard and Indiana Jones in the same section, eh?) The difference was that Kierkegaard wrote that you create the bridge yourself by taking that first step or leap of faith. The very act of stepping out into the unknown with no guarantee of success is what creates a bridge to the future and to the possibility of a positive outcome.

Alan Watts, Anglican priest and Buddhist scholar, said: *Faith . . . is an unreserved opening of the mind to the truth, whatever it may turn out to be. Faith has no preconceptions; it is a plunge into the unknown. Belief clings, but faith lets go . . . .* The Bible puts it in a different way: *Faith is the evidence of things unseen.* (Hebrews, 11:1)

A LAZY MAN'S GUIDE TO SUCCESS

At first, when you pursue your dream, it only exists as your fantasy, your vision, your own private sense of things. You are delusional. There is no evidence for your dream in the world. Others may well think you crazy, grandiose, silly, etc. for even thinking you can accomplish your dream. Your job is to get the world to share your delusion. The best way to create a reality on this planet is to get physical evidence of its truth. So your task is to step out into nothingness and create a road. Get physical evidence—awards, money, a résumé of your accomplishments, an office, endorsements or praise from others, brochures, books, recordings or other physical artifacts—of your success so far. You need something to show others you have accomplished something in order to create more agreement that your dreams are coming true or at least are realizable.

Don't let this intimidate you. You are going to start small. Remember Gordon Parks only had that one photo after messing up all the others. But that one was good. That one photo opened the door to the next place he was to go and being able to gather more evidence to show the world.

Have faith in yourself and the universe, especially when things look bad. As long as you keep taking action, you will eventually start to pile up successes. The more successes you accumulate, the more credibility and agreement you will get from the world and the more others will want to sign on to help you realize your dream (oh, yeah, and the more other people will work to thwart and undermine you, but we dealt with that above).

I once heard a story about Pablo Picasso. Near the end of his life, Picasso learned to write checks for almost every purchase he made. He had discovered that his signature was so famous that people would often not cash the check he had given them because his signature was worth more than the amount of the check. Picasso had gotten the world to agree that a little squiggle he made was worth a lot of money.

So your last task is to start to accumulate more and more evidence in the world that convinces other people that your delusion is reality. You can have a soulful obsession, follow what gives you bliss or what pisses you off, and develop your own unique way of doing it so well that no one else could do what you do, but it won't mean diddly-squat if you don't get other people to sign on to your dream. And unless you are independently wealthy, to ultimately pay money for what you do. At first, you don't have to get paid for it or even figure out what your career will look like; you just need to follow the scent of it. But in time, keep your eyes, ears and nose open for opportunities, alliances, supporters, clients, customers or venues that will pay you to bring your work out into the world.

When I decided that I was meant to teach workshops, no one walked up to me and offered to hire me to teach one. What actually got me started was that I went to a workshop back in 1977 and it was so terrible that I got pissed off. I had paid $25 (a significant sum for me in those days) for the workshop. I knew more than the workshop leader about the subject, it turned out. Worse than that, he hadn't prepared his material. Worse than that, I had driven two hours to attend the workshop on a work night. All the way home, I ranted about all this to the colleague who had accompanied me.

She just listened sympathetically. But when I arrived home and began ranting at my roommate and best friend Michael about how I could have done that workshop for half the cost twice as well, he challenged me: "So, why don't you?" He had me. But I had no clue. We had some acquaintances who had just started a graphics/printing company. The next day, we visited them. I was so flaky and disorganized that they had to walk me through every step. *You need to find a place to hold the workshop, Bill.* Oh, yeah. Where would I find out about that? *Well, people usually do them in churches or community halls or hotel conference rooms.*

The workshops I had attended were usually in hotel rooms, so I decided to pursue that direction first. After a few phone calls, I found a hotel room that I could rent for $40 for the day. I reserved it. I went back to my printer friends. *You need to write a description of the workshop.* Oh yeah. *You need to decide how much to charge.* Uh-huh. *You need to find some names or a mailing list to send people your brochure.* Okay.

Looking back, I can't believe how inefficient I was, but I didn't stop. I didn't know about mailing lists, so I just used the Social Services directory from my local mental health center and hand-copied the addresses onto my brochures. It took several nights and cramped hands. I also went around to other mental health centers and agencies and asked them if they would give them to their staff members or hang them on their bulletin boards. Amazingly, 20 people showed up at the workshop (which was about the topic that the other presenter didn't know as well as I did). I didn't lose money. I thought I didn't do very well, but the people who attended the workshop told me they liked it and wanted me to do another, more advanced one.

I was very shy at the time, but I was passionate about my subject. So, I just stood up there being nervous. My fear was just there. I told people in the seminars about it (in case they hadn't noticed my shaking voice). They seemed sympathetic and once I had warned them I was nervous, the nervousness seemed to drop down a notch or two. I was nervous for about the first 300 workshops I taught (then I guess those nerve cells must have burned out, because as I head toward my 1000th workshop I don't get nervous anymore). *(Don't let your fearful feelings stop you.)*

I just stood there and talked at first. But by reading the feedback forms and talking with people who attended, I gradually learned that I needed handouts (*That way we can pay attention to what you are saying and not have to take notes.* Okay). I also found out that I should show videos or do demonstrations to illustrate the specifics of what I was teaching; that I should use a little humor; that I should include some exercises, etc. Slowly (and I mean slowly), I began to get better and better at teaching. *(Let the world teach you. The only way it can teach you is through your taking action.)*

It took me a long time to get the logistics of marketing together. I kept handwriting the mailing labels for years. Then someone suggested that I write one set of labels and copy them onto other labels. Incredible! Then someone else suggested computerizing the list. Brilliant! Another person told me that mailing lists were available for rent. Wow! (What a lame-o I was.)

Luckily, I had also decided that I was so lame at organizing my own workshops that I had started taking actions to get other people to sponsor workshops and pay me a fee. I had initially just organized workshops in my local area. Then I got friends and family members that I wanted to see who lived in other parts of the country to agree to field phone calls and take registrations for me for workshops I would do in their cities. I regularly began teaching in Seattle, Anchorage, Phoenix, New York City, Kansas City, Omaha, and Des Moines. After awhile, I had all these brochures and began to send them to people who sponsored workshops in the therapy field. Most of the time, I didn't hear anything back. But every once in a while, someone wrote or called back, having the impression that I was well-known because I traveled and taught so widely (I sent them every brochure from every workshop I had ever done and they probably assumed it was just a sample). I also volunteered to edit a newsletter for a therapy approach about which I was excited. It paid nothing and took lots of time, but it helped me to make lots of contacts worldwide. *(Keep taking actions in the area that compels your interest. Don't worry at first about making money.)*

I also created a workshop calendar in that newsletter and began listing my workshops along with those of better-known people in that specialty. A guy in England got the newsletter and called to hire me to do a series of workshops there. When I returned home, I could now say to people that I was an international workshop presenter. That impressed them. (Hell, it impressed me!). I began to get more and more workshop offers from around the country and internationally. I started to get more confident and better at delivering them. I applied to a large national conference to teach and when I returned home, the organizers called to tell me that I had given one of the best-rated workshops at the conference and they were amazed because they had never heard of me.

Same deal with books. After a few years, I decided that those who influenced other people in the therapy field write books. I certainly had something to say. But there were a few problems:

1. I was a terrible writer

2. I was too antsy (some might say hyperactive) to sit down and write. It bored me; and

3. I didn't know anyone who had written a book and had no idea how to get one published.

Other than that, it was going to be a breeze. I sought the advice of a colleague whose career was more advanced than mine and he told me that I would never get a book published without an M.D. or a Ph.D. (I have a master's degree) because the field only respected those degrees. That hit me hard for awhile. I had been bored in graduate school and was anxious to write, not return to school. After I recovered from his discouraging helpful hint, I decided that he might be right but I wasn't going to give up without trying. Within two years, I had two books out. Writing them was torture and the first drafts were awful. But I just kept revising them and getting my literate friends and colleagues to read them. I suggested that they read my books as if I were their worst enemy and they were determined to find every logical flaw or inconsistency as well as badly-worded sentences. They complied, only too well. I licked my wounds and took every criticism seriously. (Remember, make mistakes and get feedback from the world.) The books got better. I learned more about writing. I went on to write or co-write 28 more in as many years (and still no Ph.D. or M.D.). You are reading number 30. Number 18 got me on Oprah and sold pretty decently. I used to hate writing them. I love to have written, I would say. (Don't like to write? Thanks for sharing. Sit your butt down and write.) This is the first book I have actually enjoyed writing. Took me many years, but I am finally getting the hang of this writing thing.

Now let me tell you about another of my soulful obsessions, one in which I have failed miserably so far. It stands in stark contrast to my success in my psychotherapy and writing careers.

I write songs. I love music and have been writing since I was a teenager. I don't really want to be a performer, but I would love to have my songs performed by others and be heard widely around the world. But so far, most of you reading this have never heard one of my songs, and certainly not on the radio. Some of my songs are good enough to be on the radio. But what I do with my songwriting bears no resemblance to what I have recommended to you in this book.

A LAZY MAN'S GUIDE TO SUCCESS

First, I decided that I was too shy to approach producers or performers and play my songs for them. I thought I should have recordings of them, but I didn't really have the money to go into a studio to record them professionally. So, I put it off, gradually buying instruments and recording equipment as I could afford it, so I could make the perfect recordings. This has taken many years.

Meanwhile, the world goes on without hearing my songs, without telling me which ones suck or who I should connect with to get them recorded. I have missed years of valuable learning, humiliation, making contacts, making adjustments, writing better songs, etc. Finally, I got some recordings that I liked and sent them out to a few places. No replies. I was hurt and discouraged. I stopped sending them out for a year or so. Then I tried again. One reply. I didn't hear anything special in these songs was the terse comment. I was crushed. I stopped sending out songs for another year. And so on. You get the picture. Why aren't my songs on the radio? If you have read this book this far, you know exactly what I've done wrong.

I'm ending the chapter with this story to illustrate that we're all capable of success, we're all capable of failure and we're all capable of success and failure at the same time. So let the story of a failed songwriter be a cautionary tale. This stuff won't work if you just read it and know it. It only works if you take action. I've told you everything you need to know. It's up to you now. You'll either do it or you won't.

One of the early readers of this book remarked when he read the phrase "massive actions" at the beginning of this chapter, he got scared. He suggested that I tone it down a bit, that perhaps "small and easy actions" would suffice. I considered it. But in the end, I decided, "No. I haven't seen small and easy actions work for me or for the people I have coached to success." Some of the steps you take will be easy, small and simple, but you'll probably need to take a massive number of those small steps, plus many others that won't be easy. You'll want to stop or procrastinate along the way. But if you resist those urges, take massive actions, attend to the results, and stay flexible, you will most probably get where you want to go.

CHAPTER 5. A PURPOSE RECOGNIZED BY YOURSELF AS A MIGHTY ONE: CONTRIBUTION AND SERVICE

I'm not certain about this bit, but I'll throw it in anyway. Maybe you can succeed if you just do it for money, fame, status or power. But probably not. I know that I can't.

Part of the reason that I have been so unstoppable in my therapy/writing career is that I am not in it for myself. Oh, sure, I like money and status and all of that, but that isn't primarily why I'm doing what I do. I feel as if I was called to do this work and that the world needs it. Like the Blues Brothers, I'm on a mission from God. I've felt this way from the start. So, who was I to stop when I failed? Or when I got scared? Or when I was flaky? Or didn't like to write? Get over it, my soul and God would reply whenever I would object or whine.

It wasn't about me.

I had some friends who had a folk-rock group when I was in college. They wrote a song with a line in it that I still remember. We are all flutes through which the breath of God shall pass. That's how I feel when I am teaching a workshop. I am just a flute and the breath passes through me. My task is to clean out my flute to make sure the purest tone comes through. That means I should create good handouts, prepare as best I can and make my workshops so compelling and valuable that people come away moved. My job is to keep working at my writing until my books grab people and move them.

I feel unstoppable because when I do this work, I truly feel that I am making a contribution and being of service to the world. I feel it would be selfish and indulgent of me not to keep going. The world needs what I have to give and if I don't do it, it may not get done. God is counting on me and I can't let her down.

By contrast, when I thought about being a songwriter, I felt as if I would be doing that for myself, so everything stopped me: fear, perfectionism, procrastination, discouragement, hurt feelings. (I realized only recently that this idea is silly. Music has saved my life at times. It is a noble calling and can make a contribution to the world.)

George Bernard Shaw said it well in his play, Man and Superman:

This is the true joy in life, the being used up for a purpose recognized by yourself as a mighty one; the being a force of nature instead of a feverish, selfish little clod of ailments and grievances, complaining that the world will not devote itself to making you happy. I am of the opinion that my life belongs to the community, and as long as I live, it is my privilege to do for it whatever I can. I want to be thoroughly used up when I die, for the harder I work the more I live. I rejoice in life for its own sake. Life is no "brief candle" to me. It is a sort of splendid torch which I have got hold of for a moment, and I want to make it burn as brightly as possible before handing it on to future generations.

Or here's Albert Schweitzer:

You must give something to your fellow men. Even if it is a little thing, do something for those who have need of help, something for which you get no pay but the privilege of giving.

What is it that you have to contribute to the world that no one else can? What does the world need that you can provide? Your soul and the world together will show you, if you give them a chance. You must give them a chance.

CHAPTER 6. HOW NOT TO SUCCEED

Over the years, I've observed a lot of people who have succeeded and even more who have not. I've come up with a list of the things that I've seen people do to not succeed. In previous sections of the book, I have given you ideas about how to avoid each of these traps. Here I thought I would make them explicit so you can see for sure if you have fallen into one of them.

Not knowing what you want
Here's a quote from Don Herrold: "Unhappiness is not knowing what we want and killing ourselves to get it." Yep. If you do not know what you want, you are just killing time. Taking up space and oxygen on the planet. I have a friend from my former hippie days who spends his time smoking marijuana and hanging out every day. He inherited enough money to live on, so he is not in financial need. But is he satisfied or successful? I don't think so. If this is you, reread the chapters about dreams and soul.

A LAZY MAN'S GUIDE TO SUCCESS

Choosing security over success

Greg Levoy, in his book Callings, writes that ". . .we often end up trading our authenticity for what we perceive as survival, terrified to swap security for our heart's deepest desire . . ." The poet Kabir says that most of us have this idea that salvation awaits us in the next life, but he warns that if we don't find salvation before we die, we will end up with an apartment in the City of Death, sitting around with nothing to do in the afterlife. I'm glad that the economy has changed so that most of us realize that there is no longer job security with large companies. I've worked for myself since 1981 and have felt scared and worried at times, but as the years go on, I realize that my job is secure, because I control it. No one can fire me. If I notice that people are not hiring me or buying my products, I work on changing them to make sure I still have work. Writer Richard Bach said it succinctly: "Shop for security over happiness and we buy it at that price."

If you can have faith that there is enough (enough love, enough money, enough status, etc.) instead of a scarcity of what you need, it will help you let go of security and move toward your dreams.

Being afraid of making mistakes or being criticized

"I used to think I was indecisive, but now I'm not sure."
—Anonymous

Both of these come with the territory when you pursue success. I don't know anyone who can do it right the first time all the time. A few people, like Mozart, seem to be natural-born geniuses at what they do, but most of us have to take the usual route: we have to make mistakes, practice, not know what we're doing, stumble blindly, get up, dust ourselves off, wait for the blushing to subside and then move on.

You will almost certainly be criticized and misunderstood. Sometimes attacked. Often treated rudely or unfairly or even worse, ignored. I'm not saying you should love that, but if you let that stop you, you will never get where you want to go. Winston Churchill once said: "Success is the ability to go from one failure to another with no loss of enthusiasm."

Procrastinating
Ready, ready, ready, ready, ready, aim, aim, aim, aim, aim, (you getting bored or frustrated yet?). Fire already! Get ready quickly, aim a little, then fire. Then get ready again, adjust your aim, and fire again. Or as Peters and Waterman suggested in their book In Search of Excellence, Ready, Fire, Aim, might be a better formula. Or Just do it, as the Nike ads say. Then work on getting it right.

Thinking or talking things over endlessly instead of taking action

Some wag said it well: I always wanted to be a procrastinator; never got around to it.

You do not have to process your thoughts or feelings with everyone you know for decades before you take action. Get your ass in gear and do something. Fix it in the mix, as they say in the music business. Years ago, Stuart Brand, founder of The Whole Earth Catalog, wrote that he paid attention to his and others' talk/do ratio. My former father-in-law used to say, "If you wish in one hand and spit in the other, see which one fills up first." (I think there is a cruder version of this saying, too.) They were both making the point that too much wishing and talking and obsessing are why some people do not succeed.

Justifying why you haven't succeeded

A LAZY MAN'S GUIDE TO SUCCESS

What do you tell yourself that stops or discourages you from pursuing your dreams? There are thousands of people who want to be actors, so not everyone can make it. I had obligations that prevented me from pursuing my dream. I don't have money behind me, so I can't succeed. These explanations are all potentially true, because if you believe them and stop going after your dream, they will become true. They are all good reasons for not succeeding. I'm sure you have your own variation. But they are cold comfort if what you really wanted was to succeed.

Years ago, I heard someone say, *You either get the results you are seeking or the explanation for why you haven't gotten them. The explanation is the booby prize.*

Blaming the world, other people or yourself for your lack of success

I'm not interested in who is to blame for you not succeeding and neither is the world. The world only teaches you what works when you take action towards your dream, not when you talk about who blocked you from succeeding. In the presence of blame, other people get defensive and you get discouraged. Drop the blame and move into action.

Spending your time nurturing other people's needs or dreams

You never get around to pursuing your dream because you have lots of other people—children, spouse, parents, friends—to take care of. I recently saw a TV show featuring interviews with successful novelists. Several were mothers of young children. They wrote late at night or while their children were at school. Or they took time away from their children to write. Way before he got famous, Stephen King would come home exhausted from his minimum-wage manual labor jobs and write every night. You can meet your obligations and still pursue your dreams. And watch out for obligations that you have taken on unnecessarily.

Deciding you just want to be rich or famous—period
I've met these lean and hungry people and they give me the creeps. Sometimes I've even seen them succeed for a time, which amazes me. Why can't others see what slimeballs they are? They pad their resumes. Lie and cheat. Change fields. Anything they have to do to become famous or rich. In the end, they usually drop out, I've noticed. Either other people have finally caught onto their game, or they don't have the integrity and energy to go the distance. (There is an African saying: If you shit on the road, don't be surprised to find flies on your return.) Whichever it is, I don't think fame or fortune is enough of a dream to make it in the long run.

Mind you, I'm not saying that part of your motive can't be to get money, to get laid, or to get status or fame. It just can't be your main motive. You've truly got to love what you do and it has to be genuine and contribute to the world in some way.

Grinding to a halt
"No sense being pessimistic, it probably wouldn't work anyway."
—Anonymous

If you stop pursuing your dream, it's over. If you pause, you may regroup and keep going. If you get scared and discouraged, but keep moving, you will either get there or you won't. But if you stop altogether, you definitely won't get there. Keep moving, keep experimenting, keep accruing evidence that your dream is real, keep making converts to your dreams. Even when the fat lady sings, it ain't over (that's only in opera, you know). Let 'em sing all they want, those fat gals. You just keep moving.

CHAPTER 7. THE LAZY PERSON'S GUIDE TO A LAZY MAN'S GUIDE TO SUCCESS

If you are really impatient and don't even have enough time or self-discipline or whatever to read the whole book, or, if you just want a quick review, here is the Cliffs Notes © version of my formula for success:

1. Find your soul: the aliveness, energy, passion and uniqueness that the world has tried to squeeze and shame out of you since you came out of your momma.

2. Get a dream, a vision, or a direction by following what turns you on or what pisses you off (or both). It's best to choose one that makes a contribution to the world and is not just about meeting your personal needs.

3. Take action towards realizing that vision.

4. Notice whether the actions you have taken have produced results that are moving you towards your goals or dreams. If so, do more of them until you get there. If not, do something different.

5. Take massive actions, make adjustments based on your observations of the results, vary your actions and do not stop until you arrive at your destination. I don't mean that each action you take must be big or bold. You may start with a small step, but start.

6. Do not be distracted or dissuaded from action by your feelings. Do not attend to or go with your feelings unless they are feelings that help you move forward. Have faith in yourself and the universe, especially when things look bad.

7. Create more and more evidence in the world that your dream is real so that others will believe in it too.

8. Keep moving toward your dream—no matter what. Persistence can be powerful.

I'll end with a line from the poet Rainer Maria Rilke: If I don't manage to fly, someone else will. The spirit wants only that there be flying: As for who happens to do it, in that he has only a passing interest. Are you flying yet?

APPENDIX
The Scale: Time, Money and Aliveness

When I first began as a therapist, I really paid attention to people's relationships with their jobs and money. I noticed there were many people who existed through their workday merely for the moment they could get off work and begin their lives. They lived for the evenings and weekends. That's Door #1, I thought. Do I want to take that? Others seemed to love their work, living fully both at work and at home. Door #2. I'll take that one. I want a life in which I can be alive both at work and at home. Jim Fox wrote: *My father always told me, "Find a job you love and you'll never have to work a day in your life."*

I also noticed that some people had work that didn't require their constant presence. They had figured out how to live their dream and make money without even putting forth 9-to-5 effort.

So I developed this informal scale in my mind. Here it is. You might find it useful. Keep in mind that some people can be in between numbers or mixing several numbers, so don't get too hooked on the numbers. They are just rough guides designed to make a point and show a direction.

-3 No job, no income, no fun. No way to contribute to the world through charity or service because you have to struggle just to survive.

-2 You've got a job, but it's not doing anything you like. It doesn't pay enough to cover your bills. Still close to impossible to contribute to the world through charity or service.

-1 You've got a job that you at least don't hate, but it's barely enough to live on and it isn't what you want to do with your life.

0 A job you like OK, with enough money to pay your bills.

+1 A job, maybe even a career, you really like, with more than enough money to live on. You could contribute through charity or service, but you don't have that much extra money to give or extra time in which to be of service.

+2 You love your career/job and you make so much money for doing it that you would really only have to work part-time to pay your bills. You have some time and money to contribute to others more needy.

+3 Here is where time separates from money. You make money from things that don't require ongoing activities or time, once you set them up. You write a book, a movie, a song, etc. that produces royalties. Because you have followed your passions, you invent something or start a franchise or license something to others that brings in income. You invest (well) in real estate or the stock market with the money you have earned from pursuing your passion and dream. (As I write this, the stock market is not making many people money with their money, so of course, I mean invest well after doing your homework or getting a good advisor and know that investing is usually a gamble). Your money begins to make money. (At this point, you may get another soulful obsession or find a way to give back to the world—or both.)

Obviously, you are aiming for as close to +3 as you can get, right?

Printed in Great Britain
by Amazon